ASIA

by Claire Vanden Branden

Cody Koala

An Imprint of Pop!
popbooksonline.com

abdobooks.com
Published by Pop!, a division of ABDO, PO Box 398166, Minneapolis,
Minnesota 55439. Copyright © 2019 by POP, LLC. International copyrights
reserved in all countries. No part of this book may be reproduced in any
form without written permission from the publisher. Pop!™ is a trademark
and logo of POP, LLC.

Printed in the United States of America, North Mankato, Minnesota.

082018
012019

THIS BOOK CONTAINS
RECYCLED MATERIALS

Cover Photo: Shutterstock Images
Interior Photos: Shutterstock Images, 1, 5 (bottom right), 9 (bottom left), 9
(bottom right), 10, 13 (bottom left), 13 (bottom right), 14, 17 (top), 17 (bottom
left), 17 (bottom right), 18, 19; Mel Longhurst/VWPics/AP Images, 5 (top);
Sergi Reboredo/VWPics/AP Images, 5 (bottom left); Red Line Editorial, 6;
Lucas Vallecillos/VWPics/AP Images, 9 (top); iStockphoto, 13 (top); Miro
May/picture-alliance/dpa/AP Images, 21

Editor: Charly Haley
Series Designer: Laura Mitchell

Library of Congress Control Number: 2018949680
Publisher's Cataloging-in-Publication Data
Names: Vanden Branden, Claire, author.
Title: Asia / by Claire Vanden Branden.
Description: Minneapolis, Minnesota: Pop!, 2019 | Series: Continents |
      Includes online resources and index.
Identifiers: ISBN 9781532161711 (lib. bdg.) | 9781641855426 (pbk) |
      ISBN 9781532162770 (ebook)
Subjects: LCSH: Asia--Juvenile literature. | Continents--Juvenile literature. |
      Geography--Juvenile literature.
Classification: DDC 950--dc23

Hello! My name is

Cody Koala

Pop open this book and you'll find QR codes like this one, loaded with information, so you can learn even more!

Scan this code* and others like it while you read, or visit the website below to make this book pop.

popbooksonline.com/asia

*Scanning QR codes requires a web-enabled smart device with a QR code reader app and a camera.

Table of Contents

Chapter 1

Asia

Asia is the largest **continent** in the world. It has 48 countries. More than half of all people in the world live in Asia.

Some Asian countries are partly in Europe.

Watch a video here!

MAP OF ASIA

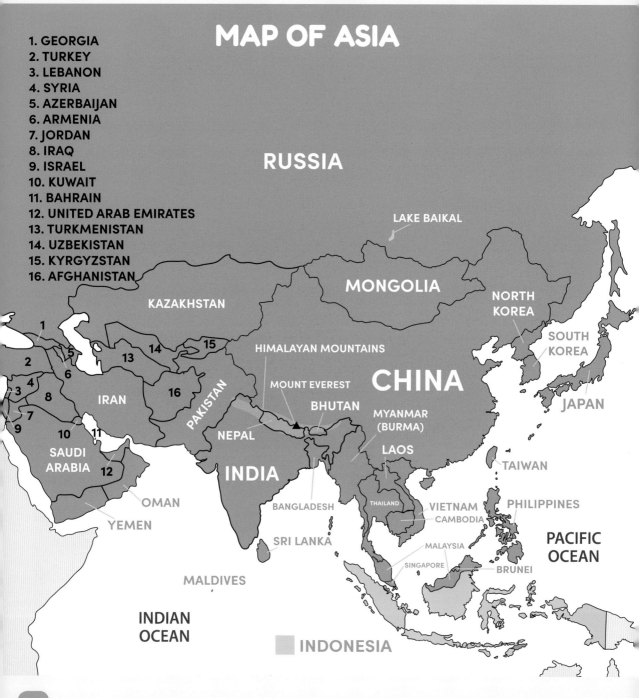

1. GEORGIA
2. TURKEY
3. LEBANON
4. SYRIA
5. AZERBAIJAN
6. ARMENIA
7. JORDAN
8. IRAQ
9. ISRAEL
10. KUWAIT
11. BAHRAIN
12. UNITED ARAB EMIRATES
13. TURKMENISTAN
14. UZBEKISTAN
15. KYRGYZSTAN
16. AFGHANISTAN

RUSSIA

LAKE BAIKAL

MONGOLIA

NORTH KOREA

KAZAKHSTAN

SOUTH KOREA

HIMALAYAN MOUNTAINS

CHINA

JAPAN

1

5
2
6
4
3   8
7   16
9
10   11

IRAN

13   14   15

PAKISTAN

MOUNT EVEREST

BHUTAN

MYANMAR (BURMA)

NEPAL

LAOS

SAUDI ARABIA

12

INDIA

TAIWAN

OMAN

BANGLADESH

THAILAND

VIETNAM

PHILIPPINES

CAMBODIA

YEMEN

SRI LANKA

MALAYSIA

BRUNEI

PACIFIC OCEAN

SINGAPORE

MALDIVES

INDIAN OCEAN

INDONESIA

Asia touches the Indian Ocean, Arctic Ocean, and Pacific Ocean. The biggest Asian country is Russia. The smallest is the Maldives. The Maldives is a group of islands.

Chapter 2

Tropical and Cold

The **climate** is different across Asia. Northern Asia can get very cold. Parts of southern Asia are **tropical**. The Middle East has hot deserts.

Complete an activity here!

Mount Everest

Mount Everest is the world's largest mountain. It is part of the Himalayan mountains in Asia.

The Caspian Sea in Asia is the world's largest lake.

Lake Baikal in Russia is the deepest lake in the world.

Animals and Plants

Asia has many different animals. Tigers, elephants, and monkeys all live in Asia. So do camels, wolves, and many birds.

Learn more here!

Asia has many forests and **rain forests**. Bamboo grows in Asia. Giant pandas eat the bamboo. Mangrove trees are in southeast Asia.

People of Asia

More than 4 billion people live in Asia. Each group of people has its own **identity** and history.

Learn more here!

China has the Great
Wall, a large stone wall
built a long time ago. It is
5,500 feet long.

Saudi Arabia sells oil to many places around the world. Oil is made into **fuel**, including gasoline for cars.

More than 2,300 languages are spoken in Asia!

Asia is home to some of the poorest and richest people in the world. Many in India and the Philippines are poor. Many people in Singapore are rich.

Making Connections

Text-to-Self

The weather is very different in different parts of Asia. What is the weather like where you live?

Text-to-Text

Have you read another book about Asia? What did you learn?

Text-to-World

There are many different groups of people living in Asia. This book mentions people from China, Saudi Arabia, India, the Philippines, and Singapore. Why do you think it's important learn about each group?

Glossary

climate – temperature and weather of an area.

continent – one of the seven large landmasses on Earth.

fuel – something burned to make heat or power.

identity – personality and other things that make up who a person or group is.

rain forest – a tropical forest with many different plants and heavy rainfall.

tropical – very hot.

Index

Online Resources

popbooksonline.com

Thanks for reading this Cody Koala book!

Scan this code* and others like it in this book, or visit the website below to make this book pop!

popbooksonline.com/asia

*Scanning QR codes requires a web-enabled smart device with a QR code reader app and a camera.